A Simple Place

Nicole Hadley
Sow Words Publications
978-0-578-00726-7

Copyrights ©2006 A Simple Place
Library of Congress Catalog Number TXU – 298 – 887

All rights reserved. No part of this book may be reproduced or utilized in any form or by an means, electronic or mechanical, including photocopying, recording, or by any information storage or retrieval system, without permission in writing from the Publisher.

Published by:
Sow Words Publications (Nicole Hadley)

Printed in the United States of America

"Now unto Him that is able to do exceeding abundantly above all that we ask or think, according to the power that worketh in us"
(Ephesians 3:20 KJV)

JESUS, You are my inspiration.

To:

Bernice Cauthen, Bertie Hadley,
William Hadley and Mary Hadley;

and to my *whole* family, I love you very deeply.
Thank you for being my support

CONTENTS:

A Simple Place

    A Simple Place 10

    Lost in Bliss (A Sonnet) 11

    Beyond the Backdoor 12

    How Does it Feel? 13

    Reality Check 14

    Nomad 15

His Light Brings Life

    He Is 18

    A Handful of Dust 19

    Life's A Composition 20

    A Love 21

    Let Him In 22

    There is More 24

    Forgiven or Forgotten 26

    Choirs 27

    Stay With Me 28

    Midnight 30

    Midnight #2 31

    The Good Heart 32

    Bittersweet Happiness 33

    A Rock for the Blind 34

    The Price of Life 36

I Tried to put Love on a Shelf... 37

Tomorrow 40

In This Mind

This Time Around 42

Oh Our Many Wishes 43

Red Moon 44

Who Will Tell Your Story? 45

The Hunger of Guilt 46

When Two First Meet 47

One Tree Stands Tall 49

When Seeing You Hurts 50

Earth is an Egg 51

Mind Over Mission 52

Who Will Stand? 54

Dear New York City

It Never Sleeps 57

The F-Train 59

The Cyber Circus 60

The "Ave." 61

Penny-less Joys 62

Black Hands 63

Standby 65

The Subway Samaritan 66

The Shiner 71

They Call Me "Big-Time!" 73

An Appeal to Elegance 74

A Simple Place

A Simple Place

Those navy, cool skies, shattered
With shiny diamonds;
When the beating of your heart
Is the only sound that's heard.

Winter winds rub against you
Turning your nose red;
The moon becomes your lantern
Giving you all the light you need.

To rest yourself
On an arctic, cement step;
That propels-a quick chill up your spine
As a rocket that has been launched into the air.

All is calm
Peaceful and serene;
Out here on these backyard steps.

LOST IN BLISS

Delightful as on a sandy escape,
With water as apparent as the sky;
Without any doubts or any mistakes
To a bliss that lets your spirits run high.
The pleasure of finding someone you love,
And definitely sure they love you back;
A sense of peace has landed like a dove
And a sense of rapture you now don't lack.
Oh harsh world don't take it away from me,
By never letting me forget my qualms;
Just leave me with a sense of ecstasy
It gives me peace of mind and keeps me calm.
Ecstasy surmounts a past of sorrow,
Swathes the present to forget tomorrow.

Beyond the Backdoor

The sun like warm lemonade-
Finds me sitting on the concrete curb,
gracefully lets down its bright glow
leaving me comforted and undisturbed.

The wind moves the dead, dried leaves
that litters the ground;
the dew of rain floats in the air
the scent of peace is found.

So peacefully lost in nature's scenery
nothing can break that hold,
until a fly lands on my thumb
so ignorant and bold.

Flying frivolously across my face
causing my mind to go astray,
from nature's splendid surroundings
wasting time shoeing him away.

Aggravating as they are
flies call Earth their home,
just as I am able to do,
they're allowed to fly free and roam.

I adore sitting in the midst
of God's creation,
such a magnificent masterpiece
that brings a time of peace and no frustration

HOW DOES IT FEEL?

How does it feel?
Like time has stopped completely,
and all I can see is myself.
My beating drum is the only sound I hear.
My mind opens up like the top to a glass jar…
and takes me away from reality;
as a balloon that has slipped from a child's grasp
and now floats into the eternity of sky.
Where words float around me,
in a galaxy full of metaphors, similes and paradoxes,
molding them together to create,
beautiful odes, sonnets, or even a prose.
How does it feel?
Immensely soothing, yet at the same time, overwhelming!
But when It's completed,
and my pen can no longer write
I look down at that flattened piece of wood-
And say "I'm finished"

REALITY CHECK

Things I once sought after,
I no longer desire.
Years have brought
a new mind and a new way of thinking.
Desires fade from material to reality.
Things that will better my heart,
and mind and will bring joy to my soul.
I now long for the things
that will leave memories,
leave marks of joy and happiness.
That will bring me a smile,
when my life has reached a storm.
These will be the memories,
that will become the umbrella
I need, to get through the storm.
It will be the blessing,
That will put a smile
On my face – when the storm has ended.

NOMAD

I'm about to go and
migrate to another nation,

make my home there
to escape this complication.

Don't need a green card
I'll just find a boat,

sail across the Atlantic
in my pursuit of hope.

Find cover while
crossing territory lines;

so swift my moves,
I would be hard to find.

Show up at the local
markets, shops, and stores;

playing as a resident
acting as if I've been here before.

Quickly adapt to
their lifestyles and ways,

treat it as my way of life
and not just a phase.

Alone,
I will be-at first,

but I'll make a living
and collect my worth.

16

I'd rather be in a land
where I'm a strange face,

then reside and dwell
in a dying place.

America is beautiful-
America is great;

chanting these words
while America disintegrates.

HIS LIGHT BRINGS LIGHT

He Is

He is the breath that gives me life
        every morning when I wake;
He is that warming comfort
        that glistens on top of lakes.
He is the blue sky
        covering me wherever I go;
He is pure like the white clouds above
        and the fresh winter snow.
He is my Moon-
        my lantern in the darkness of night;
He is my shining star
        always shining bright.

David called Him His Shepherd
so I am His sheep;
For His love runs
forever deep.

A Handful of Dust

Before the day that I was completed
I was mounds of dusty, redundant dirt;
ignored and unseen–I was not needed,
the wind oppressed me–for I was not pert.
With just a bundle of Earth in Your Hands
You became a sculptor and molded me;
I became your composition called man,
and I was made in the Image of Thee.
You gave me life from the air that You breathed
then placed me and granted me *the* control;
fenced by Your creation–to which we cleave,
as a Father teaching son to console.
Permitted us to be fourth in Your chain;
as to never let us forget Who reigns.

LIFE'S A COMPOSITION

Life is a painting that is movable
it's a spiritual masterpiece,
a work of art-
that all eyes can feast

Not made to be kept hidden
but made for Earth,
life is so beautiful
that it's not sole but gives birth

Life breathes breath
life has taste,
life has touch and sound
life even has a face

Life was made
from such a Marvelous Image,
an Image that was here from
the beginning of life and when it's finished

Not created with acrylic on canvas,
that a painter would make,
life is more like a unique sculpture
that's fragile-but can not break.

A Love

A Love that gives you everlasting comfort
As a warm embrace that never ends
A Love that won't leave you in the dirt
Like those you call your friends.

A Love that is so enormous
It's more than twice the Earth's size
A Love that's hard to comprehend
To a human's eyes.

A Love that is forgiving
To everyone's sin
A Love that has never perished
Since the beginning until the end.

A Love that will never let us down
But is always there to uplift
A Love that gave us His only Son
This was His wonderful Gift.

Now who on Earth has a love like Him?
That gives you more than red roses and carnations?
There is no love on this Earth
That can give your soul salvation.

Let Him In

Most will step into the sanctuary
finding hope and burdens set free –
come in with sorrow stricken pains on their backs,
but exit with a happy glee.

What if I told you that you can find Him,
at the place you rest your head?
the place where you bend your knees at night,
before you go to bed.

For He wants to dwell inside your heart,
while His Spirit overcomes your soul –
knowing for sure that Our Father
always will have full control.

Having His Love inside your heart –
is as an attraction of a bee to honey;
the way a wealthy heart –
would feast after money.

You with Him – connect like a chain,
you and His Spirit combined;
without knowing He will transform
your heart, soul, and mind.

Some view His Word as a text book
instead of letting It pour into their heart;
while others share a bond with Him, so strong
that they would die if they would part.

They place their feet into His Holy house
and rest their back against His pews,
cause it is their weekly tradition
that they were taught to do.

If you would lift your heads,
and widen your eyes
you too can be Blessed,
by His wonderful, everlasting prize.

24

THERE IS MORE

People don't want to believe 'cause they don't like religion. God isn't found in religion instead He wants a relationship. People refuse to give up their way of life to do what is right; becoming afraid to go against the normal – requiring you to do everything opposite of what their peers are doing.

What for? Why stand out, when you can fit in.

Truthfully, they rather be another regular; another number in the population living in America. Trying to obtain that perfect car, house, career, the list goes on...

But is that all you want?

To just *live* a life that everyone else is pursuing?

What will separate you?

Fame?

Fortune?

Intelligence?

Yet, they can only last but so long.

When you get them...what's next?

When you get all the things you longed for...then what?

Get more stuff to fill you up, just so you could be *happy*?

Yet when those things fall out of style or become outdated-or unable to work, you buy something new...

Inevitably, you'll just keep buying new things; to try and keep you happy.

Like a child who longs for a toy, or a piece of candy, knowing that after they receive that one toy or that piece of candy, they will be happy.

Until they see another kid with a different toy that looks more appealing than theirs, now they want it!

You desire what you can see…but that is tangible.

Desire more…

Desire what you can not see;

for that you live and work harder for,

because you want to know it more.

Something that you can not know fully at once,

but must grow to know.

So what else is there?

There is God.

Forgiven or Forgotten?

It's an emotional hold
that's kept locked tight;

it's covered by smiles in the day
but attacks minds at night;

Sneaks up like shadows
in the depth of dark;

hovers over your body
leaving disdainful marks;

The word alone
may seem right at the time;

but not having it forgotten
is why it pops up down the line;

Some things that are forgiven
must soon be forgotten;

Or they will become roofed by lies
that harvests feelings-to make them rotten.

Choirs

Your melodies consume my mind
and cause my feet to dance;

The way sixty mouths
can make one note,
and obtain the same tune.

Your voices are like hot apple pies,
whose aroma immediately fills a room.

Through this chain of praise
you bring Him in our presence.

The sun can pass through – yet
your voices make time stand still.

Allowing us to sing through another day

Stay With Me

I was loosing each day, wanting to give in –
having the urge to agree with my sin.
That all began from a thought that emerged;
instead of fighting it, I quickly submerged.
Freely opening my mind, to worldly desires
wanting to fulfill them-burned my brain like fire.
I walked around, acting as if I were fine,
but inside, I really wanted to unwind.
I've waited so long, to hear from Your voice
impatience kicked in and I chose my own choice
I was fed up with repeated pain and rejection;
unable to see myself or recognize my reflection.
I felt as if I was becoming whom I am not,
yet unwilling to fight and move from that spot.
I reached a point where it seemed okay,
to give up and embrace my own desire and way.
Setting aside my truth and my walk –
tempted to erase it all, like chalk.
For once I desired the things I kept away
things that would harm me, and later would pay.
So lost, I began to feel inside –
as if I was stepping away from Your Eyes
The pain ate at my inner wall –
Fighting, yet determined not to give up and fall.
I looked to You for healing to my soul
although I was angry, You still have control.
Eager to feel for the Love we share;
my soul now needing a new repair.
Through the shadows I sought Your light,
You came to me – when I was heavy with plight.
I heard you speak, although quite low to hear,
"Stay with Me", is what You whispered in my ear.
My burdens left, and my shoulders grew light
In awe how You brought me back in one night.

You Love me when I'm not looking your way,
You give me strength Jesus, and with You I will stay.

Midnight

Midnight is our darkest hour
all alone – awaiting God's Power.
To drain out the sin we've been drowning in –
broken, hurt, and scarred
but He's there to mend.
Knees grounded to the cold floor
eyes shut, tears streaming
unable to take anymore.
Daily the world tries to snatch us up,
spit us out, left to die with
an empty cup.
While in the dark you sit there –
down on your knees
head hanging low,
awaiting for the Lord to ease.

Midnight #2

Midnight – our darkest hour
opposite of noon's light
which gives us power.
The Light which shines on the dark
to make it seen,
open up our hearts to reveal the things
that are unclean.
Just let it be
because God already knows what's inside –
even though He has to get us alone
to bring it to our eyes.

The Good Heart

I'm the one who people seek after,
and the one they struggle to be;
But the persuasion of the world – like a razor,
cuts through minds persistently.
Yet, I am that slight whisper in your head,
telling you the right way to go,
but like a sheep amongst its herd,
you instead go with the flow.
I'm the pure as sugar dove,
that can defeat a pack ravens;
although you seek trouble,
I'm the one who provides a safe haven.
When you first received sight,
I was more visible than ever,
but without notice – corruption sunk in,
like a sought forbidden treasure.
I can never leave your side,
because in you I naturally reside,
only through Love, and peace of mind,
Is how I truly stay alive.

BITTERSWEET HAPPINESS

Bittersweet happiness,
oh heart I know you've known;
you are that daily familiar voice
on the other end of the phone.

You call, when there's good news to tell;
yet always busy,
when my days are not too well.

Yet, I always forgive you.

Especially when there is no rain
when the storms have subsided,
and the sun shines over – high
and always invited.

Bittersweet you are –
for you never stay for long,
one minute I'm humming joyous melodies
and soon bobbing to Blues' sad songs.

Bittersweet you are –
because you are not forever,
you come and you go
like the ever-changing weather.

A Rock for the Blind

We have eyes you can see
although slimy to the touch,
with these pairs we witness the world
which at times can be too much.

Take everything we see
to us, appealing to be true,
for it is something we look at
and things we already knew;

Could you believe in what you can not see?
And take it as being true?
like someone saying the sky is red
when you know it's really blue.

We believe History happened
without being present in those times,
yet some can't fathom the Truth beyond this world
'cause the world has kept them blind;

Years and years we walk this Earth
partaking in what it has to give,
follow your daily routines
thinking it's the only way to live.

When your hour has come
where do you think you would go?
Do you assume it's just death
or are you too afraid to know?

Yes, at times it seems
this world has a lot to bestow,
but when you depart from it
where will your drifting soul flow?

You decided to allow this world to blind you
instead of seeking what is Truth,
preferred to eat, drink and be merry
loving the flesh of your youth;

How long will you not see
the eternal treasures you will miss?
what your body can not comprehend
but will give you soul total bliss.

Know that Jesus is the living Rock
to offer sight to the blind,
now let that reality
forever dwell in your minds.

THE PRICE OF LIFE

What is a life worth?
For some, a tangible pair of shoes,
a cell phone,
money,
fame,
and for some, gain.
But you know what life is REALLY worth?
A life.
What expresses how priceless life is, than giving up your own?
Jesus gave up His life – for every life.
That is the price of life.

I Tried to put Love on a Shelf

I tried to put Love on a shelf. High up so I couldn't see it; or even reach it. My plan was to forget about it, let it sit and collect dust. I decided it didn't fit into my life-well at least at this time in my life. Although, I was hoping maybe one day I would be cleaning and find it again; or maybe it would fall from the shelf and find me.

I hopped down from the metal step ladder and I looked up towards the top shelf. I could no longer see it but I knew it was there. I felt it in the room. I stood there gazing up at that top shelf, unable to see Love but knowing it was looking down at me.

I figured with Love out of the way it was time to do something for myself; spoil me for once! With Love, I was always last on my list. Always giving my time, affection, sympathy, talents, skills, and even my money! But sometimes the Love I wanted would not give back. Sometimes he would be silent and not say anything, which would make me so angry to the point I would break into a temper tantrum as though I were a five year old. Yet he would always give me what I wanted when I needed it. He was always on time with his gift giving.

I could not stop the smile that unwillingly appeared on my face, when I thought about the joys I had gained from him in the past. How even giving to him and others was not as bad as I was making it seem. But! That was then and now I'm just tired. No, I'm not giving up-just giving in-into myself. I don't want to be disappointed anymore. So I had to set aside the one thing that was making me feel dissatisfied and aggravated. I wanted more – I wanted to experience something new! Yet I felt that Love had offered me all I needed, but not everything I wanted.

These *things* I once dreamed for, no longer bring happiness. They have become lifeless statues that have taken up space in my life and now only served as an illusion of the company that I missed. What else could I buy? Who can make me feel better? What am I missing?

Three months I went without Love. Each dying day of those months felt as if it were pulling the very life and strength I had left in me. I thought I could replace Love with my success, my friends, my money, my possessions, and even a man! Yet even though I left him, Love had a way of being in my thoughts, in my talk and even in the people I encountered.

Three months I went without Love or so I assumed. I recollected Love's ways of maneuvering himself into my life. Even though I tried leaving him behind; I finally realized that Love was always with me. I was just ignoring him.

I rushed back to my bedroom, pulled out my step ladder, and I reached for Love again. I stretched my arms high, to reach that shelf. I rapidly slid my hand back and forth on that shelf, seeking him.

Tears of sweat slowly began to form on my forehead as I frantically sought after him. Dust began to smother the palm of hand, but I could not quit. Where was he? I stood on the tips of my toes, reaching, sweat now dripping, from my face and beads of sweat glazing my lips. I could taste my struggle; I could taste my passion for him. As I continued to reach for him, the ladder began to wobble from side to side and eventually it fell from under me. I quickly grabbed on to the shelf. Just as I was hanging there, Love fell from off the top shelf; hitting me on the crown of my head, before he and I fell to the wooden floor of my bedroom. Once on the floor, I grabbed Love as tightly as a child who was lost but found their mother. I held him so tight as to never loose him again.

- God is Love –

40

TOMORROW

Live for today-they say,
Live each day like it's your last;
for they have no control over tomorrow,
all they know of is their past.
So why build your life
around a future you have "planned"?
when tomorrow isn't promised,
only God makes those commands.

In This Mind...

THIS TIME AROUND

Have you ever let time slide?
Let it flow through real smooth;
cancel your responsibilities
and just let your heart groove.

When every minute passing
was more like an hour;
even time to gaze
a full blooming of a flower.

It's a desired feeling
every soul wants to devour
the only antidote
to cure them of being sour.

Flip this pencil over
and erase stress, anger, and pain,
for this moment –
everyone is diagnosed: sane.

OH OUR MANY WISHES

I wish I could see how I think.
If I did, I wouldn't have such inane thoughts.
For my thoughts would be visible,
for everyone to see.
But then my thoughts could be exploited
through the misperceptions of what people see.
They'll know what is happening is true!
Because what they're seeing is coming straight from my mind.
There will be nothing I could hide from them.

Wouldn't that be better after all?

Then there will be no more secrets to be kept hidden;
all doors will be open;
lies will be extinct.
Yet, there will be nothing
to make someone want to know me,
for they will already know me before I even speak.

What a world it would be.

RED MOON

Red moon – did you see it?
How much time will they waste denying You?
Denying You exist?
When the very essence of who they are,
breaths their Creator.
How long will they keep on their blindfolds?
How long will they allow their intelligence
to deceive them – for all it is, is human knowledge.
Human knowledge that's foolishness to God
and it will surely pass with this world.

Repent. Know HIM,
before you are fooled by those perceiving to be Him.
His Love is freely given –
we did not earn it;
we did not even deserve it;
so why deny a Love so sweet?
Yet you continue to eat, drink, and do as you please,
making yourself become ignorant
by your own wayward wisdom.
Digging a pit for your very soul to lay in – to die in.

So…did you see it?
Did you see the Red Moon?
I saw it–
He's showing us the signs,
that Day is coming soon.

WHO WILL TELL YOUR STORY?

Days drift into the setting of the sun
night falls, while a new day is set to come.
Time soars, into the eternity of the sky
yet you're standing here, and don't know why?

Who will tell your story?
Would anyone care to know?
would your life be memorable,
before time lets you go.

Some dream of a life lived well,
some for fame and some for wealth;
pursuing a path of fame,
to gain a name for their self.

How do you want to be remembered?
has it ever been asked?
Have you ever thought
that maybe, your name could last?

Who would tell your story?
Who would care to know?
Would your life be memorable?
before time lets you go.

THE HUNGER OF GUILT

It's hard to hide its raging tunes
whose din of shame consumes the room;
her enemies all well aware
you, her friend, let loose her despair.
Your mind plotting your pending doom
for sharing secrets before her tomb.
Together you both walked inside
she aloof to the scornful eyes;
it seemed at once-they all had grinned,
holding back their contempt within.
So unaware, she was-your friend;
whom to her you were more as kin.
Raged as acid against an empty wall,
wishing she could rewind it all;
act as if it never occurred
the secret she told, was never heard.
"Oh Time, why do you run so fast?
I'll give it all up-to have my past!"
Pointless pleads that drifted in air,
only Truth could make it all fair.
Instead she plans to just pretend
to tell-may lose her only friend.

As the creatures in the still night,
she craftily hides her horrid plight.

When Two First Meet

It's funny how my heart beats uncontrollably
when my eyes take a glimpse of your face,
It is as if love has captured me
in an unseen embrace.

Yet so tranquil you stood
calmer than a summer evening's breeze
unaware of the anxiety you were putting me through
that grew higher than the trees.

You must have felt my eyes
because in an instant – they met
you made your way forward
while my stomach felt tangled in nets.

*It's funny what love can make you do
like stare at someone
when you know at the time
you ought not to.*

*It's like my heart is in control
and has outwitted my mind
for you had my heart
in an un-detachable bind.*

*Wondering what would you think?
if you looked back and met my eyes gazing,
would you turn away with disgust
or would you find it quite engaging?*

*What if you knew I waited for you,
everyday, when you went out to leave?
would you find that romantic?
or would you be quite displeased?*

48

*Yet today – you gleefully looked my way
and I headed in your direction
hoping that you too
would share the same affection.*

Nonchalantly I fixed my clothes
dusting off my apprehension
also trying to come up with words to say
not to mention.

Then there you stood
eye to eye and toe to toe
yet a word did not seep out –
Nervous, I was,
and flushed without a doubt.

Our eyes never left their gaze
it was as if they've met before
love rained out my body
and even through my pores.

There we stood – silent
but our eyes were talking just fine;
it was as if the world had stopped
and love was controlling time.

ONE TREE STANDS TALL

I am the branch that took
Thirty-three years to grow;
My leaves just beginning to bud
For there's things I still need to know.

Storms rage against our timber
Yet we stand firm and strong;
For this love runs thick
And has the strength to last years long.

Greed like lightening
Causes many to crumble and burn;
Their eyes protruding with envy
Looking upon us with yearn.

Moss takes toll over our beautiful trunk
Too weak to defend against age and seasons;
Rotting too soon – I thought
But I will never know the reasons.

You are our base – lifting us high
so we too may share your light;
Until the Earth lets you go
and takes you away into that Great Night.

WHEN SEEING YOU HURTS…

Your once strong, sturdy body,
walked with ease and quickness;
I would have to take two GIANT steps
just to keep up with your one.

Gave birth to four children
the third blessing was my mother;
your eyes watched her, like they watched me.

You fed us with your lively pastimes;
and always kept our ears urging and wanting
to gobble up your stories.

But now…well now…seeing you hurts.
That once strong body began to whither,
like a strand of hair placed over a light flame.

Your quickness faded into timid tiptoes,
that paused every two feet
before reaching your destination.

Your mind that once held a library of the past,
could not even remember one book.
Placing the past and present,
on the same plate – made sense to you.
Now realizing that you now need
the care that you once gave me.

EARTH IS AN EGG

Earth is an egg
waywardly wobbling to and fro
unsure if it's destination and
where it wants to go.
It's tip shows its power
while its bottom shows it's truth;
how the wealthy are few-but on top
dominating our dense and hurting youth.
Has a hard shell,
yet quite gentle,
and easy to be cracked;
because we protect it with pride
when Love is what it lacks.
While inside lies its slimy,
mess of confusion,
destruction, hatred, and death;
people just living an illusion –
oblivious that Earth
does not have much time left.

MIND OVER MISSION

It's an everyday battle
far beyond what I can see,
for this unending battle
resides inside of me

It's this war that sheds
my brother's blood to the ground,
wondering why I'm still breathing
when death is occurring all around

I came to fight on soil
that is not my own,
some of my fellow men know why
as for me-the reason is unknown

Yet I signed my life
on that white sheet of paper,
totally unaware of what or where
I would end up later

To be able to once again
rest my head at my home,
where I can feel the hands of those I love
to be comforted and not alone

But…they trust me to watch them
so they too may rest their heads,
to prevent the hands of death
from attacking them in their beds

Now I'm battling in a war
between my heart and my flesh,
one's telling me to stay
while the other wants out of this mess

To just find a secret path
and stake my way out,
leaving everything behind
including my doubts

The moon is my lantern
'cause even the sun has to sleep,
like my fellow companions
whose eyes are closed when I weep

Use what you hold
is the advice my mind gives,
telling me the weapon I hold
is what will help me to live

All it takes is one shot
aiming at myself,
easy like that-I am discharged
and I gain back my wealth.

WHO WILL STAND?

The Economy…

If I hear that word one more time I think I'm going to scream; grab my hair in both hands and grit my teeth until I feel better. Who's to blame? Who should we point the finger at? Bush? Well, that's who everyone wants to point their fingers at. But wait…isn't America a democracy? So where were we with our picket signs and protests to end the war? Why didn't we ALL stand up and dispute against our President's commands? Hmmm…makes you wonder. If we who proclaimed, "united we stand, divided we fall", why didn't we stand together as a Nation to demand a change?

Yeah, we all agreed the war in Iraq was pointless while we watched updates about it on the 10 o'clock news; or when we gathered around the water coolers at work; or the times we chatted with a friend about it over the phone. So why didn't our complaints make it past the comforts of our homes? Yet we leave it to the heartbroken mothers who have lost sons and daughters on that battlefield; or to the wives left to raise up infants; and to the brave but few young adults who protested outside of where the President laid his head.

Where is that revolutionary spunk that sparked a protest in California against the war in Vietnam, in the Sixties? College students were struck with tear gas and gun shots from their own fellow Americans. Where is that drive to stand up and combat against what is wrong? We just let it subside, let things decay just like this…economy (Ahhhh!)

DEAR NEW YORK CITY...

It Never Sleeps…

Whether by wheel

or by rail,

whether by water,

or by feet,

they make their way to the City.

Where edifices reign

looking down on its many pedestrians

who flood the City's streets,

mainly by feet,

trying to make it

in this City that does not sleep.

Finding it a treat

to be apart of this City's beat.

Making their bodies slaves

to it's lifestyle

digging their minds a grave;

for they've lost all sense of who they are.

Feeling it is better

to race the streets –

dodging in and out of people

when you really have plenty of time!

Dashing across at GREEN lights –

trading a few extra minutes for your life!

58

Just to work in a City

that does not sleep:

that's always open,

whose candle is always lit,

the bulb that never dies.

But you…

you need sleep,

so why compete?

With a City that does not sleep.

THE F-TRAIN

A frightening ride to freedom,
so exhilarating your blood pressure rises,
your nervous heart beats like a Congo drum.
What is that rhythmic thump I hear?
is it the wheels hitting the rigid tracks
or my size 8 ½ foot tapping the floor in anxiety.
The train nervously shakes from side to side,
moving faster and faster,
keeping steady as if afraid to break its stride.
Bringing me to the next chapter of my life,
not stopping until our destination is met;
introducing me to new level of excitement and strife.
New personalities to love and to clash,
new times to cry and to laugh.
Where my independence will constantly be in thought,
sometimes my individuality will be fought,
By the time I get there my mind will be drained,
riding on this frightening, free, and fast F train.

THE CYBER CIRCUS
(A PARADOX TO THE TEXT MESSAGE)

"The Cyber Circus" is the place that demands more of you than time itself. When answering a text message becomes more important than making a call. When text-ing a friend, *what are you doing?* – is more important than reading a book. Or what about the times when you're stuck piecing together a choppy story through a one-inch screen because the text-er could not fit every word at one time. Thus, you end up having to call them anyway because you have no idea what they were talking about.

Isn't that the purpose of the cell phone anyway? To talk not read! However cell phone companies make it much cheaper for you to text rather than to talk!

Cell phones are the ring leaders. Branching from in-car cinderblock shaped devices, to pocket-sized picture snapping, internet-having, technical pests. People can't go anywhere without it. They *must* be able to be reached wherever they are, even if they're in the bathroom.

And oh how sweet they make those cell phones sound – with their Blackberries and Chocolates. Who knew a phone could taste so sweet? We have become the elephants, the tigers, the seals, being manipulated to perform in the tricks they have designed for us. Waywardly attempting to pull us deeper and deeper into their plots, tricks and plans to brainwash us into believing we need those technical gremlins.

So I ask you, Ringleader, what's next? Cell phones planted in our ears?

THE "AVE."
(AN ODE TO JAMAICA AVE. IN QUEENS, N.Y.)

This outstretched valley –
over powered by shops and stores,
some may hate it, but some others adore.
Grime embedded streets
everyday succumbed by people's feet,
who are trying to buy themselves a treat,
while hoping their pockets do not seep.

Walking down the brick paved sidewalks
it's like walking on history;
but its impenetrable streets
are what hides the mystery.

PENNY-LESS JOYS

Yeah, money may be a stranger to my pockets
or to a wallet that is non-existent,
but how would you know that?
For I walk among you
and can even talk like you do,
yet you will never know,
I did not have a permanent place to rest my head.

While you dress yourself in pinstripes
and silk dresses-
I dress myself in a smile, that was given
by a joy that will never be removed.
A joy more expensive than all the pleasures you can buy,
Its is a joy for those
who the world has offered them nothing.

"Though you have not seen him, you love him; and even though you do not see him now, you believe in him and are filled with an inexpressible and glorious joy"

- 1Peter 1:8 (NIV)

BLACK HANDS

Sir,
will you please let me wash your hands?
The hands that are stained with
the grit and harshness of this world;
for they hold so much history – a story to tell.
But they've been covered with thick,
charcoaled layers that have smothered your hands
to the point they can not breathe.
Most look upon you and turn away with disgust
feeling as if their eyes were too precious,
to even take a glance at your presence.
Yet, you still see them as possible donors,
and make way towards their turned backs.
But when you came to me,
you caught my full attention – even though I had company.
Your hand gripped your stomach,
your clothes were torn and tattered,
your coat once held the beauty of forest green,
but now portrayed a rusty gray.
The hair on your head, draped over your face and ears.
Yet your shagged hair revealed
a peak of your face – a portrait of hurt,
hunger and struggle;
Your lips parted to speak – only 2 teeth were shown.
You told us you hadn't eaten in 3 days,
all you wanted was some money,
to get something to eat to ease your hunger.
I wanted to give you more
than the quarter that I so happened to find
in my coat pocket, but it was all I had.
You reached out your hands,
and I dropped the shiny quarter on top of your
charcoaled, blackened hands.
You gratefully thanked me

and slowly walked from my presence.
If only I could wash you hands sir.
To see the dirt and pain that this world,
has thrown on your back, be washed away.
Let it stream back into the soil,
from which it came.
How do we let our own be subject,
to find comfort in places where rats,
make their homes?
Is this not the land of opportunity?

STANDBY

He waits in anticipation
like he did the first time;
making a bed on the New York streets
just to be first in line.
With one leg strong
he waits…
as the night air deepens fast;
he just buttons his coat,
looks at his watch
and is happy that he isn't last.
Five-hundred strong
plus this night,
which brings him to five-hundred and one,
after he sees this show,
he'll still never be done.
He's made himself notorious;
they branded him,
their biggest fan
so honored to be appreciated,
by such a delicate, fragile man.
Every Saturday they bring him to 'his'
designed seat,
as he sits back and enjoys life,
engaging in this treat.

THE SUBWAY SAMARITAN

The heat from the sun penetrated through his bedroom window, that wintry morning. It blazed through his skin and eventually seeped to his bones. He tossed through the bed sheets to move out of the sun's rays. He forfeited to the sun and decided to just get up – although his alarm clock claimed he had another half hour of sleep left.

With eyes still closed he sat up, crossed his hands, and thanked God for another day. With this extra time, he thought he would make breakfast; let the aroma of bacon and grits float throughout the home – and wake up the rest of his family. Breakfast, 15 minutes and the alarm still had not gone off yet once. He set the table while three mummies appeared into the kitchen. He knew the breakfast would wake them up. Not often did he get the opportunity to sit and eat breakfast with his family during the week. Every time the opportunity came, he never let it pass. It always seemed like the world was always calling his family to be somewhere else.

Having the opportunity to talk to his family before work was something he treasured. To be able to hear his youngest son rant in excitement about the stars and the planets, while trying to shove down a strip of bacon at the same time. While his eldest just sits back, in awe of this wonderful breakfast. Time called them back to reality when he looked at the microwave, and realized it was time to get ready to go. It seemed like minutes later he had his sons by their hands, making their way down the grit-stained stairway, of the 1-Train subway stop. The walls matched the stairs – for they shared the same grim and acute scent. It wasn't their fault that the city doesn't care to clean their stations; knowing that it is corroding with aged dirt from millions of the feet, garbage and waste.

As they waited for the 1-Train, he noticed a young college aged man, staggering across the platform. He was caught in awe over the fact that no one else seemed to notice, even though he stood out like red lipstick on a white cotton blouse.

He watched the young man carefully as he staggered waywardly from left to right – he wasn't drunk – more like unconscious to his surroundings. He whispered to his boys to stay put, then ran over to aid the young man. The young man was convulsing, his peach-like tone began to fade to pale. Two women scurried over – one put a plastic spoon in his mouth to keep him from choking. The other woman left to go outside to call for an ambulance. Moments later the young man continued to stagger on the platform, not even seconds passed when he soon tumbled his way onto the subway tracks. The man knew it was up to him to continue to help the young man. So he calmly hopped down from the subway platform and onto the tracks, being careful of where he landed, not wanting to touch the third rail.

He cautiously lifted the young man trying to get him on his feet, so he could lift him back up on to the platform. Due to the young man's unconscious state his body became lifeless pounds weighing the man down, and making it almost unbearable to lift the young man on to his feet.

As he continued to lift the young man, he noticed that the puddle of water in the middle of the tracks began displaying rings, and soon the rings turned into fast ripples;

"The train is coming!" one of the women called from the platform. In haste, the man began using every bit of strength he could muster; trying to pull back the strength he had when he was twenty years old. He finally got the young man to his feet, but by that time he already saw the headlights from the 1-Train approaching. . He knew he did not have enough time to lift this young man back on to the platform. So instead he threw the young man down into the large gap in the middle of the tracks and then laid himself on top of the young man; and in seconds the 1-train, passed right over them. The man did not even breathe the whole time he laid underneath the 1-Train. He could smell the hot metal from the wheels of the 1-Train; the smell almost suffocating him. It felt as though the train was going to devour him alive, the way it covered him. Minutes passed, and so did the train. The man did not move until the train was no longer in sight

When he stood, he wrapped the young man's arm around his neck and carried him to the edge of the platform. To his surprise no one got on that train. Instead they helped pull the young man back up on to the platform. The men patted him on the shoulders and commended him for his bravery. He nodded in agreement,

"Somebody had to do it."

"And I'm glad you did." One of the men chimed in. Afterwards he signaled for his two sons to come back in his direction. Each took hold of their father's hands; the youngest looked up and stared into his father's face in awe. Through his eyes he saw a real-life superhero; unlike any that he watched daily on television. This superhero was his father.

"All thanks to you." they said.

"And God!" the man proclaimed strongly

"Yes, there is a God, because what just happened today was surely a miracle for that boy."

"In fact sir, may we get your name and address?" one of the officer's asked. The other looked at his fellow officer with slight confusion.

"Well, my name is Samuel Marcy…but wait, what do you need with my name and address?" he asked.

"Well, your act of courage in helping that young man, surely deserves a reward." the officer replied.

"There's no reward needed; the reward for me is that that young man is still alive."

"If you had not taken that step, who knows what could've happened to that young man."

The man nodded, shaking their hands in gratitude,

"Thank you both. I am just glad that I was here to help him, and mainly that he's alright."

"Are you sure?" The officer said, already folding up the paper in which he had already written his name, and placing it into his back pocket.

"Yeah I'm sure. God has ways of rewarding me. I'm just glad that he is okay" he replied, looking behind the shoulder of the officer, noticing the next train approaching, "but now, I have to take my sons to school."

They watched as he eased by them as well as the other people who had witnessed the whole incident. When the train stopped he got on and sat down facing the door, where the police officers and onlookers stared at him, as the automatic doors slid close – and the train took off.

(Modern day miracles)

The Shiner

He sits and he waits.

With a freshly cleaned cotton rag in his right hand and a can of shoe shiner in the other; both hands rested on his lap.

He waits.

Tired and stressed, he yawns, and allows his watery eyes to slip down his cheek, covering up the real tears that fell. He waits.

Looking down at his own shoes that were so tarnished and worn, he could no longer revive them. A quick shine could not remove those stains. People walked by but very few looked in his direction, yet knew he was there. Some looked at him with expressions of pity and shame.

Yet he still waited.

The train station had been his second home for a decade now and he could not fathom how he allowed it to last that long. With agony in his eyes – he waited.

"Excuse me! Regular shine please!" a man garbed in a black suit and blue tie demanded, looking down at the man.

"Have a seat" the shoe shiner replied, with a forced smile; he then began working on his first customer of the day.

The man pulled out his newspaper and created a barrier between them, not wanting to spark any kind of conversation.

The job was done, the money exchanged and he was back sitting at the foot of the chair…waiting. Waiting for that hour, the hour

72

in which a change would occur in his life; for a new day to unfold. To one day have his shoes shined.

They Call me "Big Time!"

They call me "Big-Time!" because I was chosen to be apart of their money-hungry sect that each day adds layers and layers of unwanted, superfluous stress, that builds and builds as the years progress. They call me "Big-Time!" because I have to garb myself in suits–some dazzled with pinstripes, preferably not my type–but just right for them. So everyone can see how my success has stemmed.

They call me "Big-Time!" because I hang a degree upon my wall, so high up and firmly placed that it could never fall, so everyone can see my call...it is success after all. They call me "Big-Time!" because my slip has three extra zeros than most, which would make some people want to boast, have a party and be the head of a toast.

They call me "Big-Time!" because I'm young and have conquered the success of this world; able to afford both diamonds and pearls; everything is wrapped around my finger like a curl. However this new name, the nickname that charges me with wealth and fame, putting me in a class where the rich reign; but how come this "Big-Time" feels nothing but pain?

If I set it free from me, leaving the career where money flows free, with a price that deducts years from my life - will I still have the name? The name that stains me with fame?

An Appeal to Elegance

Beauty engaged her as she made her way down the red velvet carpet. She lifted her left palm over her face as a shield against the flashes of bright lights that consumed her – almost blinding her vision. She was accompanied by many others who were paid to be in her presence.

Once inside, smiles greeted her; along with hugs and handshakes. Familiar and unfamiliar faces received the same greeting as she followed her fellow guests up the marble stairs, and into the enchanted ballroom. The yellow glow from the crystal chandeliers lit the entire room with such splendor; while the white covered round tables circled the freshly waxed wooden floor.

Classical jazz played in the midst as she was brought to her table, marked *Reserved*. She was shown to a seat where her name was placed on a tag, typed in gold letters that in the light's reflection would shine. She sat down in the midst of her party, still displaying her pearly white smile. Once settled she slowly began to fade.

At the table they conversed about work and how beautiful the gala was, while reminiscing on past successes of the company - which she stood before.

Model-like gentleman dressed in white, with white

napkins neatly placed over their right forearms, brought out their dinner. They gave each person a plate consumed by, fillet mignon, freshly seasoned green beans, and garlic mash potatoes. Choices of wines were placed before her; she chose white.

Dinner was finished and the tables were soon empty again. The jazz band began playing some fast tunes as everyone, now slightly intoxicated, began getting loose and letting the music take control of them. Yet, she sat still at the table and gazed at all the excitement from her seat. She began looking at her watch, hoping that the time would move faster than it was. Two familiar faces embraced her presence and sparked a conversation. Afterwards they encouraged her to get up and dance a little, but she gracefully declined.

Later, she was compelled to get up and at least prance around in her gown that was surely luxurious. She slowly strolled about the room, in a way for her luminous gown to catch the attention of those she had not greeted. But, only a few approached her. So she started making her way back towards her table to sit in the only chair that was designated for her, for the night.

Was this the only way through; the tunnel leading her to complete happiness? Everyone's ultimate dream was just a false reality to her. She had every worldly desire in her possession, yet still had to force a smile.

About the Author

Nicole was born and raised in New Jersey. She began writing at the age of nine, and with much encouragement from others it has become a long lasting passion of hers. She is a graduate of St. John's University in New York. Through her writing she hopes to enlighten, encourage, and overall share the Love of God. "May these words of my mouth and this meditation of my heart be pleasing in your sight, LORD, my Rock and my Redeemer." (Psalm 19:14).

Thank You!

I hope you enjoyed reading *A Simple Place*, and were touched by the book in some way!

To find out more information about upcoming books or to send your feedback, please contact Nicole at:

nicolehadley08@gmail.com

www.ingramcontent.com/pod-product-compliance
Lightning Source LLC
Chambersburg PA
CBHW051713040426
42446CB00008B/862